It's Easy To Play Cat Stevens.

Wise Publications
London/New York/Sydney/Cologne

Exclusive Distributors:
Music Sales Limited
8/9 Frith Street, London, W1V 5TZ, England
Music Sales Pty. Limited
27 Clarendon Street, Artarmon, Sydney, NSW 2064, Australia

This book © Copyright 1984 by
Wise Publications
ISBN 0.7119.0577.X
UK Order No. AM 37904

Art direction by Mike Bell
Cover photography by Peter Wood
Arranged by Cyril Watters
Compiled by Peter Evans

Music Sales complete catalogue lists thousands of
titles and is free from your local music book shop,
or direct from Music Sales Limited.
Please send 50p in stamps for postage to
Music Sales Limited, 8/9 Frith Street, London, W1V 5TZ.

Printed in England by
Eyre & Spottiswoode Limited, Margate, Kent.

How Can I Tell You

Words and music by Cat Stevens

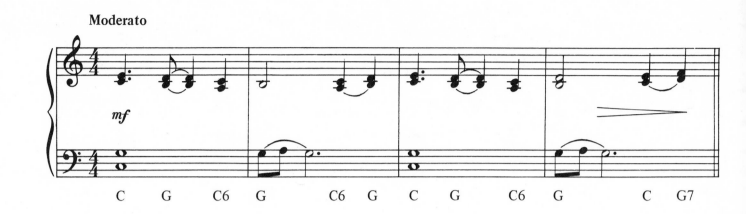

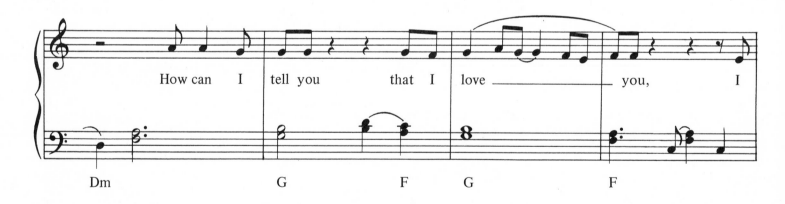

I long to | tell you | that I'm | al - ways think - ing _ | of you, | I'm

Dm   G   C   F

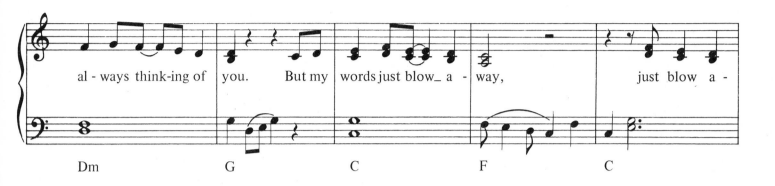

al - ways think-ing of | you. But my | words just blow_ a - way, | | just blow a-

Dm   G   C   F   C

way.   It | al - ways ends up to one | thing hon-ey, and I | can't think of right words to

F   Dm   F   G   C   F   C   F

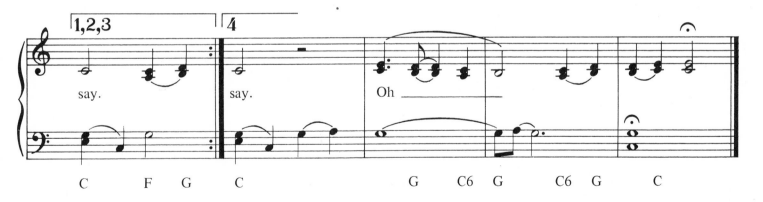

1,2,3   **4**

say.   say.   Oh ____

C   F   G   C   G   C6   G   C6   G   C

2.   Wherever I am, girl,
         I'm always walking with you,
         I'm always walking with you,
         But I look and you're not there,
         Whoever I'm with I'm always,
         I'm always talking to you,
         I'm always talking to you,
         And I'm sad that you can't hear,
         Sad that you can't hear,
         It always adds up to one thing, honey,
         When I look and you're not there.

3.   I need to know you,
         Need to feel my arms around you,
         Feel my arms surround you,
         Like sea around a shore.
         I pray in hope that I might find you,
         In hope that I might find you,
         Because hearts can do no more,
         Can do no more.
         It always ends up to one thing, honey,
         Still I kneel upon the floor.

Bitterblue

Words and music by Cat Stevens

Fairly bright 4

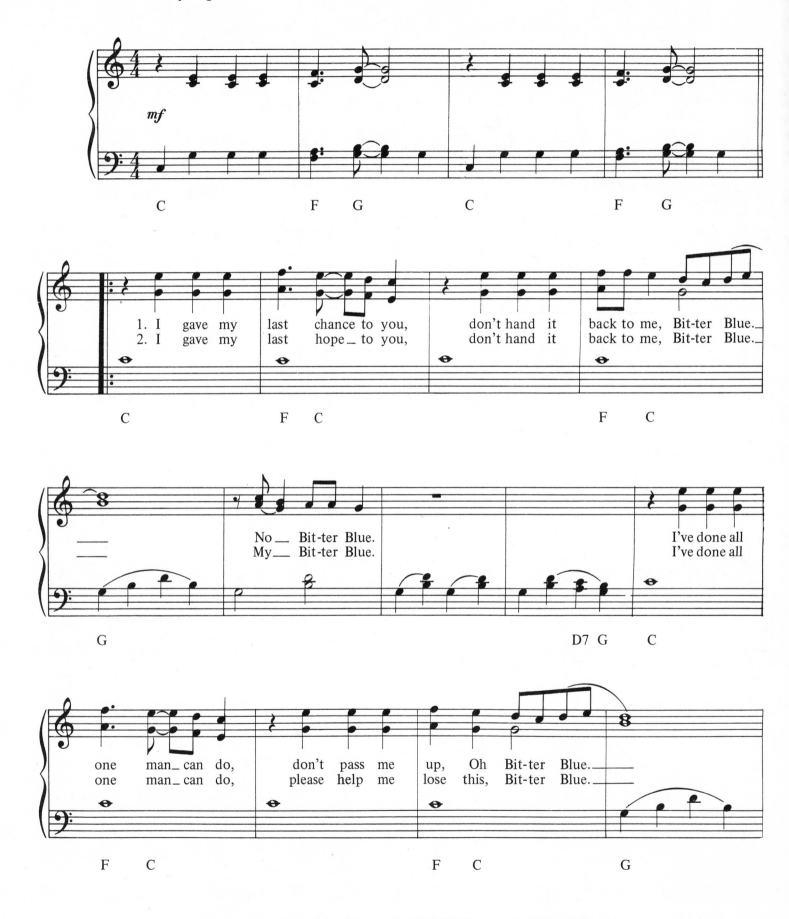

Wild World

Words and music by Cat Stevens

Can't Keep It In

Words and music by Cat Stevens

Steady four

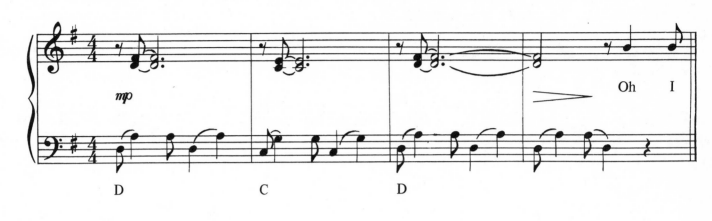

D   C   D   Oh I

can't keep it in,   I can't keep it in, I've got-ta let it out.

G   C   G   D   C   D

I've got to show the world,   world's got-ta see,   see all   the love,

C   D   C   D   C   D

love that's   in me. I said,   why_walk_a-lone,   why wor-ry when it's

G6   D   G

warm ov - er here. You've got so much to say,

D   C   D   C D C

To Coda ⊕

say what you mean, mean what you're think - ing and think an - y - thing. Oh

C   D   C   D   D   C   D

why, _____ why must you waste your life __ a - way, __

G   C   G   C   G   Em

_____ you've got to live for to - day, __ then let it go. __

A7   D   G   F♯m

Oh _____ lov - er, I want to spend this

A7   G

13

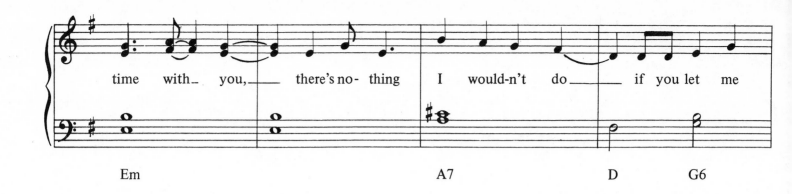

time with you, there's no- thing I would-n't do if you let me

Em   A7   D   G6

know.   And I can't keep it in,   I can't hide it and I

F#m   G   C   G

can't lock it a - way.   I'm up for your love,   love heats my blood,

D   C   D   C   D   C   C   D   C

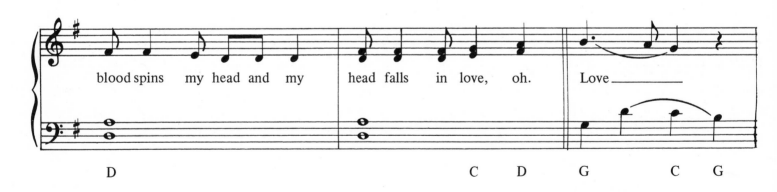

blood spins my head and my head falls in love, oh. Love

D   C   D   G   C   G

That's no way to live your life, you all - ow too much to go by,

                        Em   A7

and that won't do,_____ no _____ lov-er.

D   G6   F♯m   A7   G

I want to have you here by_____ my side, now don't you

Em

D.𝄋. al Coda

run, don't you hide._____ while I'm with you. 'n' I

A7   D   G6   F♯m   D   C

CODA

(Spoken)

think an - y -thing, why not?_____ Now, why, why, why not?

D   G   D

C   D

If I Laugh

Words and music by Cat Stevens

2. If I laugh just a little bit
   Maybe I can forget the plans
   That I didn't use to get you
   At home with me alone.

3. If I laugh just a little bit
   Maybe I can recall the way
   That I used to be before you
   And sleep at night and dream.

Hard Headed Woman

Words and music by Cat Stevens

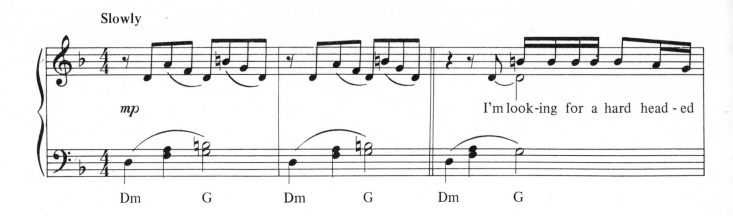

one who'll make me do my best,— and if I find my hard head-ed

Cm   F   Dm   Am   B♭   C

To Coda ⊕

wo - man, I know the rest of my life will be blessed, yes, yes, yes. —

F   B♭   C   F   Am

— I know a lot of fan-cy dan-cers, Peo-ple who can glide you on a

Dm   G   C   Cm   F

floor.— They move so smooth but have no ans - wers,—

Dm   Am   B♭   C

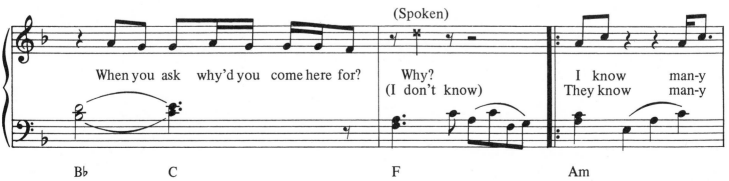

(Spoken)

When you ask why'd you come here for?   Why?   I know   man-y
                                          (I don't know) They know   man-y

B♭   C   F   Am

19

fine feath-ered friends but their friend-li-ness de-pends___ on how you do.
sure-fired___ ways___ to find out the one who pays___ and how you do.

D   Am   D   F   E

I'm look-ing for a hard head-ed wo-man,

A   Dm   G   C

One who will make me feel so good.___ And if I find my hard head-ed

Cm   F   Eb   Dm   Am   Bb

D.%. al Coda

wo-man, I know my life will be as it should, yes, yes, yes.___

C   Gm   C   F   Am

CODA

rall.

Dm   G   Dm   G   Dm

20

Lady D'Arbanville

Words and music by Cat Stevens

A tempo

La - dy   d'Ar - ban-ville   Why does it grieve me

(Em)   D

so?   But your heart seems so si - lent.

                                                          Em

Why do you breathe so low,   why do you breathe so low?   My
                                                                      2. I

D   Bm   G   Em

La - dy   d'Ar - ban-ville   why do you sleep so
loved you   my la - dy,   though in your grave you

(Em)   D

still?   I'll wake you   to - mor - row
lie,   I'll al - ways be   with you,

22   Em   G

why do you sleep so still? I'll

wake you to - mor - row And you will be my

fill, Yes, you will be my fill. La, la, la, la, la, la.

La, la, la, la, la, la.

La, la, la, la, la, la, la, La,

D   Em

D

Bm   G   Em

D   D7

Em   G   D

Sitting

Words and music by Cat Stevens

To Coda ⊕

27

3. Oh I'm on my way, I know I am,
Somewhere not so far from here.
All I know is all I feel right now.
I feel the power growing in my hair,
Oh, life is like a maze of doors and they all
Open from the side you're on.
Keep on pushing hard, boy; try as you may,
You're gonna wind up where you started from.

Moon Shadow

Words and music by Cat Stevens

Fairly slow

To Coda ⊕

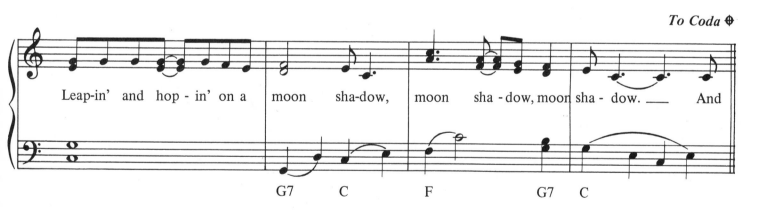

if I ev - er lose my hands, Oh if _____ I
if I ev - er lose my eyes, Oh if _____ I

F   C   F   C   Dm   G7   C   E7   Am

1
won't have to work no __ more. _____ And

2
more. _____ Yes, I'm be-ing foll-owed by a

Dm   G   C   C   C

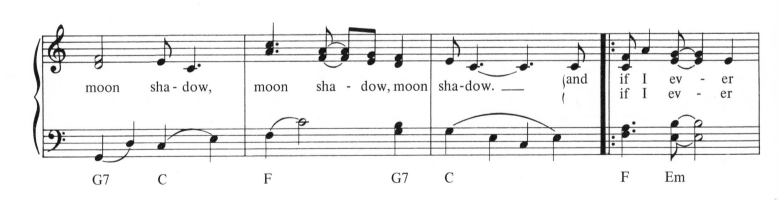

moon sha - dow, moon sha - dow, moon sha - dow. ___ Leap-in' and hop - in' on a

G7   C   F   G7   C

moon sha - dow, moon sha - dow, moon sha-dow. ___ (and if I ev - er
                                                        if I ev - er

G7   C   F   G7   C   F   Em

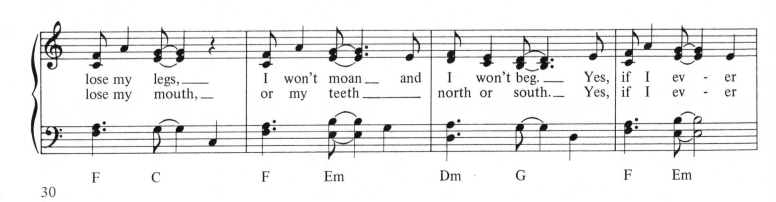

lose my legs, ___ I won't moan __ and I won't beg. __ Yes, if I ev - er
lose my mouth, __ or my teeth ___ north or south. __ Yes, if I ev - er

F   C   F   Em   Dm   G   F   Em

lose my legs, ___ Oh if _____ I won't have to walk an-y
lose my mouth, ___ Oh if _____ I

F   Em   Dm   G7   C   E7 Am   Dm   G

1

more. _____ And won't have to talk. Did it take long to find me?

mf

C   Dm   G   D7   C D7 G

2

I asked the faith-ful light. _____ Did it take long to

D   C   D   G   D7   C   D7

D.%. al Coda

find me? _____ And are you gon-na stay the night? _____ Oh,

G   D7   C D7 G

CODA

Moon sha-dow, moon sha-dow. ___ Moon sha-dow, moon sha-dow. ___

F   G7   C   F   G7   C

31

Father And Son

Words and music by Cat Stevens

It's not time to make a change, just re-
time to make a change, just sit

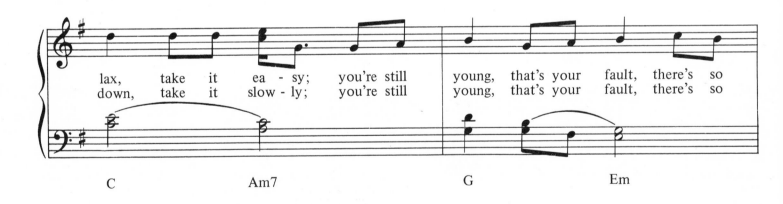

lax, take it ea - sy; you're still young, that's your fault, there's so
down, take it slow - ly; you're still young, that's your fault, there's so

much you have to know. Find a girl, set - tle down, if you
much you have to go through. Find a girl, set - tle down, if you

To Coda ⊕

33

do, he turns a - way a - gain, It's al - ways been the same, same old sto - ry. From the

C   Am7   G   Em   Am   D7

mo - ment I could talk I was or - dered to lis - ten now, there's a way, __ and I know that I

G   Bm   C   Am7   G   Em

D.%. al Coda

have to go a - way, I know I have to go. It's not

D   G   D   G

⊕ *CODA*

them, they know, not me, now there's a way____ and I know that I

C   Am7   G   Em

have to go a - way, I know I have to go.

D7   G   D7   C   G

Tuesday's Dead

Words and music by Cat Stevens

Quick four

1. If I make a mark in time, I can't say the mark is mine.

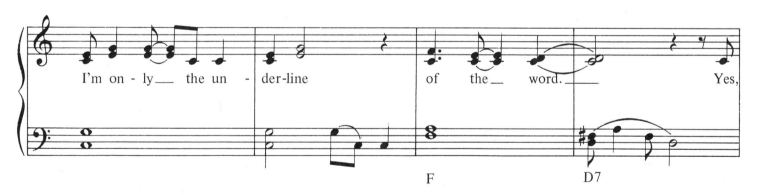

I'm on-ly the un-der-line of the word. Yes,

I'm like him, just like you. I can't tell you what to do. Like

ev-'ry-bod-y else I'm search-in' thru what I've __ heard. __

F   Am G C

Whoa, __ where do you go when you don't __ want no-one to know?

F   C   F   C G   C

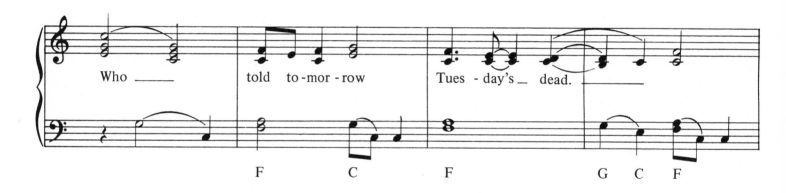

Who __ told to-mor-row Tues-day's __ dead. __

F   C   F   G C F

1,2   3

2. Oh   3. Now ev-'ry sec-ond on

G   C   (F)   G   C

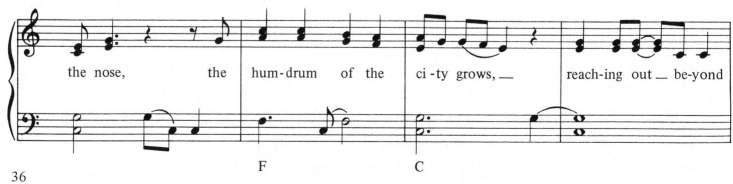

the nose, the hum-drum of the ci-ty grows, __ reach-ing out __ be-yond

F   C

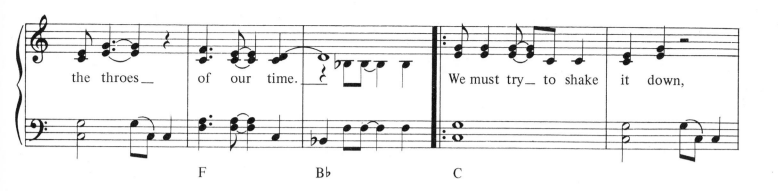

the throes of our time. We must try to shake it down,

F   Bb   C

Do our best to break the ground, Try to turn the world a - round one more

F   C   F

1. time. 2. time. Whoa, where do you go when you don't want

G C   G C   F   C   F   C

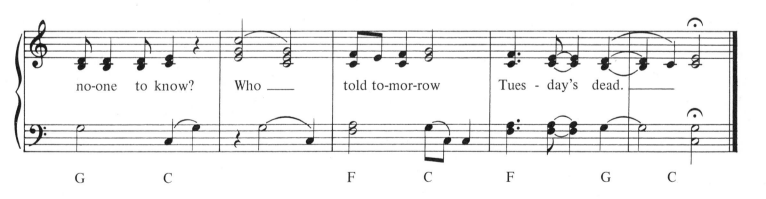

no-one to know? Who told to-mor-row Tues - day's dead.

G   C   F   C   F   G   C

2. Oh preacher won't you paint my dream,
Won't you show me where you've been,
Show me what I haven't seen
To ease my mind.
'Cause I will learn to understand
If I have a helping hand,
I wouldn't make another demand, all my life.
Whoa — where do you go when you don't
Want no-one to know
Who told tomorrow — Tuesday's dead.

3. What's my sex, what's my name?
All in all it's all the same;
Everybody plays a different game, that is all.
Now man may live, man may die,
Searching for the question why,
But if he tries to rule the sky — he must fall.
Whoa — where do you go when you don't
Want no-one to know
Who told tomorrow — Tuesday's dead.
Now every second on the nose,
The humdrum of the city grows.

Morning Has Broken

Words by Eleanor Farjeon
Musical arrangement by Cat Stevens

Moderato

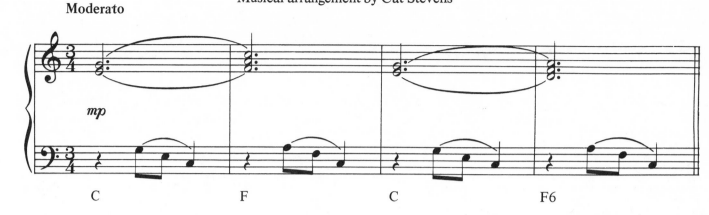

C   F   C   F6

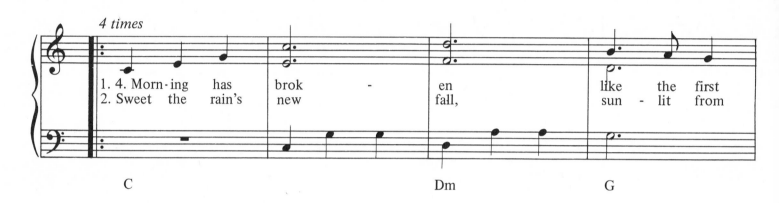

4 times

1. 4. Morn-ing has brok - en, like the first
2. Sweet the rain's new fall, sun - lit from

C   Dm   G

morn - ing.   Black - bird has spo -
heav - en.   Like the first dew -

F   C   Em

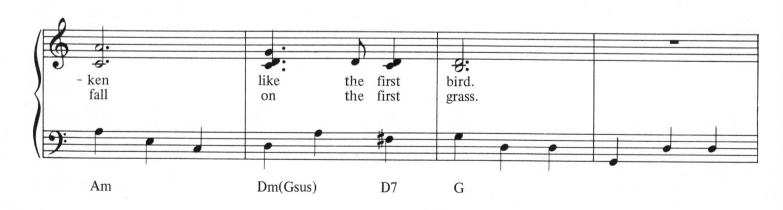

- ken   like the first bird.
fall   on the first grass.

Am   Dm(Gsus)   D7   G

3. Mine is the sunlight,
    Mine is the morning,
    Born of the one light
    Eden saw play.
    Praise with elation,
    Praise ev'ry morning,
    God's recreation
    Of the new day.

Lillywhite

Words and music by Cat Stevens

Sad Lisa

Words and music by Cat Stevens

Where Do The Children Play?

Words and music by Cat Stevens

make them tough, but they just go on and on and it seems that you

C   Dm   C   Bb   F

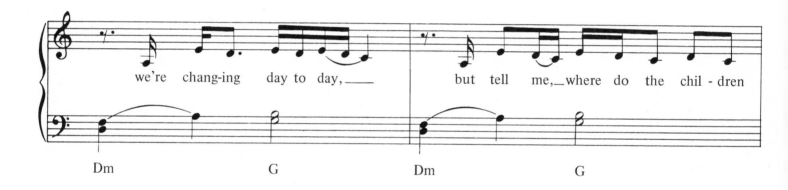

can't get off.   I know we've come a long__ way,__

Bb   F   Dm   G

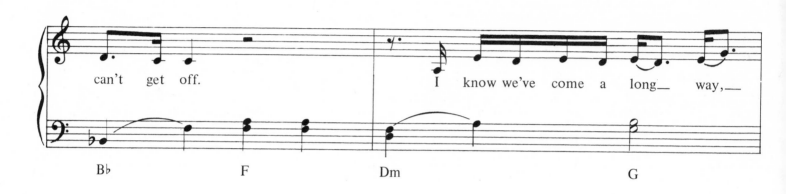

we're chang-ing day to day,__   but tell me,__where do the chil-dren

Dm   G   Dm   G

play? __

C   Dm   C   F   C   F

Well you've cracked the sky, scra-pers fill the air; but will you

C   G   C   F   C   Dm   C

keep on build - ing high - er till there's no more room up there. Will you

F   C   Dm   C

make us laugh, will you make us cry? Will you tell us when to live, will you tell us

Bb   F   Bb   F   Bb   F

when to die? I know we've come a long way, we're chang-ing day to day, ___

Bb   F   Dm   G   Dm   G

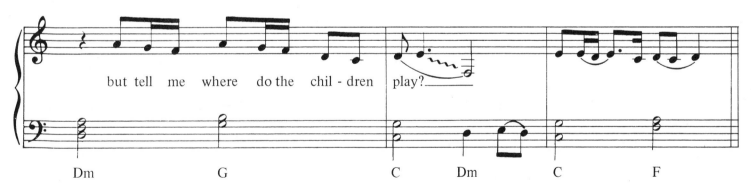

but tell me where do the chil - dren play? ___

Dm   G   C   Dm   C   F

Repeat and fade

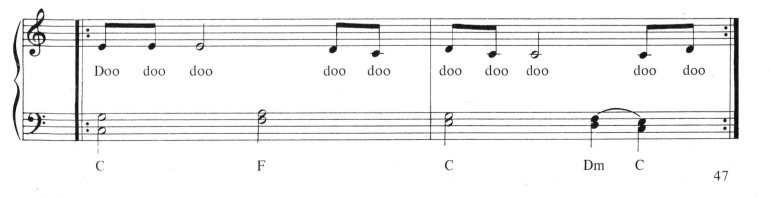

Doo doo doo doo doo doo doo doo doo doo

C   F   C   Dm   C

47